S0-GQE-902

ADVENT
DAY BY DAY
IN THE HOME

by

Liselotte Nold

and Gisela Harupa

Illustrated by Willi Harwerth

Translated by Omar Kaste

OMNIA VINCIT VERITAS

THY WORD IS TRUTH

AUGSBURG PUBLISHING HOUSE

Minneapolis   Minnesota

ADVENT DAY BY DAY IN THE HOME
Copyright © 1962 Augsburg Publishing House
All rights reserved.
Library of Congress Catalog Card No. 62-17507

Published originally by the Church Women of Germany
(Mutterdienst)
Publisher of original German edition: Laetare-Verlag, Nuremberg, Germany.

Scripture quotations are from the Revised Standard Version of the Bible, copyright 1946 and 1952 by the Division of Christian Education of the National Council of Churches.

Music reprinted from *Hymns and Songs for Church Schools*, copyright 1962 Augsburg Publishing House.

MANUFACTURED IN THE UNITED STATES OF AMERICA

FOREWORD

During the past years there has been a growing concern in rela-
tion to the observance of Advent. Christians feel the need for a
spiritual preparation for Christmas in addition to the usual shopping, sending of greeting cards, baking, and the countless other
activities associated with the Christmas season. This has resulted
in requests for materials to be used in this preparation.

Advent Day by Day in the Home will answer the needs of an
individual or a family as they spend some time daily looking forward to the birthday of Jesus. It is a translation from the German,
originally prepared from articles by Mrs. Liselotte Nold and Mrs.
Gisela Harupa, both associated with the Bavarian Mutterdienst
(Service to Mothers) of Stein, Germany. We are indebted to Mr.
Willi Harwerth for the interesting illustrations. To all these persons
we are most grateful for their willingness to share this material
with others.

The Lutheran Women's Coordinating Committee of America has
been responsible for making this material available for publication.
May all who use it receive a rich blessing from the messages and
inspiration it contains. May it prepare its readers for a new spiritual
experience during the days prior to Christmas.

DOROTHY HAAS
*Director, American Lutheran
Church Women*

First
Sunday
in
Advent

Children love Advent calendars, with their many mysterious little windows and doors. We had one in my childhood home. How wonderfully exciting it was to open one of the little windows, every morning to see something new, every morning to be a little bit closer to Christmas! The time remaining until Christmas Eve always seemed to us to be too long to be imagined. We could scarcely wait to discover the mystery behind the most important door of the calendar, the one for December 24.

For grownups, and especially for mothers, matters are generally just the opposite of this. The days and weeks before the holidays go by much too quickly and are not long enough for everything which still has to be done, for all the preparations which yet have to be made. In fact, many adults actually dread this ordeal called Christmas. Even though this is an Advent calendar for grownups, it is intended not to help you pass the time until Christmas, but to stretch it out for you. It is meant to help you pass more peacefully and joyfully through these weeks of preparation.

Advent is one of the best times of the year—and not just for children. It is a time in which our households and families once again draw closer together. Darkness falls so quickly on these short afternoons, and more of life is lived indoors. Once more Christmas lies just ahead. There are certainly many who pretend that all of this has nothing at all to do with them. Yet, in this season all of them are more willing than usual to be with others, to celebrate, to hear and to see good and beautiful things. Then too, there are more opportunities now than ever to do good, to

4

share our happiness, and to make the Child of the Manger the center of our lives and attention. All the trimmings—the good foods, the bright lights, and the gifts—would lose their meaning apart from him.

If you care to, you can, of course, read this booklet all the way through at one time. However, it is planned like a children's Advent calendar—one page per day. No one should think that the joy of Christmas can be grasped hurriedly and at once. The very wisdom of Advent is that it gives us the time we need to prepare ourselves quietly and to grow more and more into its joy. Each day's reading in this booklet will take about five minutes. We surely can find that much time. As we do this we will be in the company of many others who are doing the same thing. We will think the same thoughts together for a while each day, now and then we will be doing the same things together, and so we will come to think of one another. And of course all of the things suggested here are meant to stimulate your own thoughts and actions in this season.

Many readers will in the course of the days discover in this booklet familiar old acquaintances: words, thoughts, and above all, the figures from the nativity scene. Do you still remember how, in those hard years after the war, Urberl, the walking shepherd with the rolled-up sheet under his arm, led us all in gathering bedding to give to those who are the best-loved brothers of the Christ child: the homeless and the poor? Many will recognize also the other shepherds and the animals, because these figures from the nativity scene have long been in their homes. At Christmas time it is good to greet the return of these familiar things. It is good that we remember and are remembered. This calendar is to help this reminiscing, this daily remembering of the great joy of the season. Our hearts are so quick to become excited, or angry, or discouraged. Joy and expectation are much more seldom attained. Yet we certainly have just as much to wait for as the children do. For God is ready to give us everything—yes, really everything.

First Monday in Advent

When we were little children, the days often seemed very long to us. I used to say to my brother, "If only Mary would come now, or one of your friends!" Then we would look up and down the street. Most of the time nobody came. Now we are too grown-up and too laden with cares to fall prey any more to that kind of childish boredom, but we still know the joy of receiving visitors. Do you remember how on some occasion in the past that kind of good news suddenly changed everything for you? Perhaps it was a telegram or a post card with a few short words—"coming on next Thursday's train"—and life took on new zest. When that happens there are suddenly so many preparations to make, for everything must be just right! All we do is done in joyful anticipation. Then comes that moment when we go to the station and wait at the gate. Finally, among all the other faces, there appears that one we have been waiting for. This joy at receiving a visit from those we cherish is a special kind of blessing, and we should receive it thankfully.

At first look, this may seem to have nothing to do with Advent. But please allow me to make this comparison, for *God came, too.* I mean the time when he sent his Son into the world. He wants to come to us now, too. He wants to meet us today, and tomorrow, and every day. And he wants to speak to us. Yes, to speak to you and me very personally. "I know how you grieve because your husband no longer loves and honors you. Once you were prettier and easier to love than you are now, he says. But do not fret yourself, for to me you are as lovely as ever, even with your tired heart and weary body."

Or God's word can be like this: "Do not listen to the many rebuffs you are given when your employer wants you to do more than you can, or to be more cheerful than your heart permits, or more clever and talented than you can possibly be. You are acceptable to me just as you are. Don't be ashamed of being tired or despondent, for you don't have to pretend with me; before me you can be yourself."

Or perhaps God speaks thus to a certain man: "You aren't going anywhere in your job. Your associates don't think much of you. Even your family is disappointed, for they had expected more of you. But I expect nothing of you except that you receive my love for you, that you see and believe that I am coming to you now."

Or perhaps he speaks like this: "You sit in the circle of your happy family, yet you are somehow alone. Everyone admires your successes, they all love your cheerfulness, but they do not know you. They love only an image of you, and you yourself they leave alone. I don't care at all about your successes, your position in life, or your supposedly happy disposition. I am concerned about you and your heart, the way it really is."

Can we truly believe that God comes and that he speaks to us in this way? He knows that it is no easy thing for us. He knows that we must be reminded continually. It is for this reason that Advent must come again and again to us, as it comes this year.

First
Tuesday
in
Advent

Today we begin making the manger scene, and a certain amount of messiness will be unavoidable. Don't let that upset you, dear housewife, for the mess is part of this ritual. But why begin this so early? Perhaps in the past you have always brought out the figures for the first time on December twenty-third and then simply put them under the Christmas tree—that can certainly be a good way of doing it. But it can be even better for everyone in the family if, long before Christmas, you will begin to build a landscape for the creche, and then, as the days go by, place the figures into it one by one. This will make it easier to remember what we came to see yesterday— that God comes to us. Seeing the manger scene in the midst of our housework, or even just knowing that it will be there when we get home: this helps us remember that God comes. Then, too, giving ourselves time with the nativity scene helps us think of improvements to make in it. Thus, without realizing it, we come to live with the story of the humble birth in the stall, and of the shepherds in the fields, and of their great fear and joy.

Now we will need a suitable table or a board with a raised edge, moss, water, sand, soil, and, if possible, a gnarled old root. It is a good idea to take all of the figures out of the box and to put them on the empty table: it makes planning easier. A good way to begin is to take your Testament and open to the Gospel of Luke. Sit down while you do it; the extra time is not wasted. There in the second chapter, verses 1-20, is the story: ". . . they laid him in a manger . . . in that region there were shepherds out in the field . . . the angel of the Lord appeared to them . . . and they went with haste." The

Christmas story tells us exactly what we want to build. Just as surely as the story stirs our hearts and hands, so surely does it rule out all distracting phantasy. Mary, Joseph, and the Child do not take their places until Christmas Eve, but already now we are preparing the most honored place for them. There must be a pasture for the animals, and a path leading from them to the Christ Child. There must be at least one tree made from a twig, and a pond made with a piece of glass will fascinate young and old. Don't forget, either, that the three kings are said to have come out of the desert. So now let's begin with it. There is no one who can't do this. Only you must decide to devote an unhurried evening to it, and not just "get it done some way." Nervous people gain peace in this way, sad ones can become more cheerful, and people without imagination have their thinking stimulated. I have seen at least one pale and harried paper-shuffler so transformed by becoming absorbed in the Christmas story and how best to portray it that he didn't even recognize himself!

Just one more suggestion: get someone to help you. If you ask Grandma for advice or ask Andy to fetch the sand in his pail, then it will become partly *their* manger scene. I know a man who looked at the scene again and again, but only because he had rigged the lighting in it. Consider together what is the best place for the sheep who is lying, and for the two who are grazing. The others will be added next week. The sleeping one will need a place which is sheltered snugly from the wind. Perhaps a stray one can be drinking at the edge of the pond. Or two might have their heads together as they graze. (One of them is always afraid of missing the better grass which he thinks the other might find.) On the whole, they should not be too scattered, so they can be watched by a black shepherd dog. And far and wide there is not a human to be seen.

9

First
Wednesday
in
Advent

Do you remember the story of Jesus blessing the little children? Perhaps it was at a Baptism that you last heard the words: "Let the children come to me, and do not hinder them, for to such belongs the kingdom of God. Truly, I say to you, whoever does not receive the kingdom of God like a child shall not enter it."

The story of Jesus blessing the little children fascinated a certain devout Frenchman. Finally he wrote down his idea of how Jesus might say it today. It goes like this:

"I love children," God says. "I desire that all people become like them. I don't love grownups unless they are still children. Further, I want only children in my kingdom—that was decided in eternity. Wizened children, wrinkled children, gray-bearded children, any kind of children you can name. But children, only children. That is irrevocable; it has been decided for good—there is no place for anyone else.

"I love little children," says God, "because they are still capable of getting bigger, of growing. They are always achieving, always on the way. A grownup, on the other hand, has no place else to go. It is a pity that grownups believe that they have already arrived. I love grown-up children because they can still struggle, and because they still commit sin. Don't misunderstand me—it is not because they commit sin that I love them, but because they admit it and because they really try not to sin any more. I don't love grownups. They have never caused anyone any pain, and they know of nothing about themselves which could be improved. I can't forgive them, because there is nothing for which they need forgiveness. It is heart-rending, to hear this from them," says God, "heart-rending because it is not true.

"Perhaps the time has come for you to let me make your face beautiful and pure and serene like a child's face. For I love children," says God, "and I want everyone to be like them."

In order really to celebrate Advent as little children do, and not only to "get through it," a mother must be willing to sacrifice. Among other things one mother "offered" the cleanliness of her window pane for four big "Sunday" stars and for many small "weekday" stars. Those children had a wonderful time. It was done in this way: they had cut the right number of stars out of gold paper, threaded them on a string, and hung them in a bunch on the window knob. Every morning it was a new child's turn to paste a star on the window. As the pane became more and more golden, inside and outside, it was easy to see how close Christmas had come. This made them all happy.

First
Thursday
in
Advent

I was a little embarrassed recently when a little child took me by the hand with this urgent plea: "Please, tell me a story!" I don't like to tell stories and I'm not good at it. Nevertheless, I believe that today we should resolve to tell our child a story, and not just any story, but the Christmas story. No one is going to listen except just this little child, and it will go better than you thought possible. The joy of getting it told will help. It would be well if you choose a time to tell it when it is no longer bright in the room, a time when you could look at the manger scene together. Give yourself these ten minutes with the child.

I know that it takes so much time and strength and money simply to provide for a child's clothing and food, and that is certainly necessary. But what will he remember of his childhood once he is grown? Just a few things: how Father scolded him, or how good the after-school sandwiches tasted, or how he ran away with his pal and refused to say where he had been—and maybe how Mother told him the story of Mary and Joseph that time. By doing that you are giving him something as important as food and drink, for you are not just telling a fascinating story but the vital news of God's love to small and great. It happened on our earth—you can find Bethlehem in any good atlas. Many think of Bethlehem as a sort of children's town. For them it falls into the same class as the Christmas carnivals of their childhood with their mysterious candles and lamplight, their sweets and ginger cookies and wonderful puppet shows. But Bethlehem is no children's city. It became God's birthplace. Children often can more quickly grasp what that means for us and our lives than we grownups can.

We should try to be like the little girl who had heard the Christmas story from her father. "Daddy," she asked breathlessly, "were there real houses in Bethlehem, with real people like us living in them?" "Yes, there were very real people there," assured her father. But she was not satisfied. "Daddy, were there fathers and little children and . . ." as she paused, her eye fell on a particularly beloved bit of reality in her young life, her brown-and-white dog. "Daddy," she continued with a deep breath, "were there dogs in Bethlehem, and birds, and everything just as we have?"

We should let ourselves catch a little of this little girl's passionate desire to grasp the reality of Bethlehem. Then we should be able to imagine that if in that night when Mary and Joseph came to Bethlehem as wanderers without a roof over their heads the homes and hostels had not been overflowing, and if the people of this city had been more hospitable than people usually are, then Mary and Joseph with their child might have found a place on, say, the second floor of No. 7 Olive Lane. Then the shepherds would have had to climb a flight of stairs, knock on the door, and ask, "Does God's Son live here?" Would it all have been as "real" as that? Yes, certainly. God has come to meet us: that is the message of the Christmas story. He came the long way from light and fullness and heaven, from eternity and joy into a little place on our earth because even today he wants to be, and can be, very near us.

First
Friday
in
Advent

I always feel a weight lift from my heart when I have sent away my Christmas packages. Perhaps you feel the same way, even though you may send only a single package. This single package can many times require as much effort as ten others. For everything depends on the content of this package.

Don't you think it might be a good idea to mail your package or packages right now? Both the receiver and the post-office workers, who are so hard-pressed during these weeks, would be glad if you did. If you simply write on them plainly that they should not be opened until Christmas, each package will become the occasion for many weeks of happiness. It can say to the one who keeps it: "Someone has remembered me."

I am reminded of a cartoon which I saw years ago in some newspaper. There was a street of richly-decorated shops. Everything glittered and shone—tinsel, gifts in every price class, Christmas trees and silvered pine branches were everywhere. On a street-corner stood the Christ Child, looking very shy. He was holding on to a policeman's hand, and it was plain that he did not dare cross the street. Underneath was this caption: "Oh, so much splendor! There is certainly no need for me here."

Looking at the Christmas displays and buying gifts together can be wonderful. However, it would be a good idea to make yourself a list beforehand, even if you find time for it only when you go to bed, so that you must put the paper and pencil on the night stand. It would be wise to plan carefully in advance how much you can spend for presents, and who should be especially remembered this year. Let us not forget the Christ Child and his place in our giving of gifts! For it is neither we nor our gifts that are most important at Christmas, and we should not be so played out and exhausted on December 24 that we no longer can celebrate. This Christmas why not send only a greeting card to someone whom you know well and who would understand? Then, in its place you could give something to some person who does not expect anything from you—to an elderly aunt, or to the nice woman you learned to know on your vacation. Perhaps you could remember that tired saleslady who so patiently helped you find what you wanted.

The important thing about gifts is neither their size nor their quantity. If only the recipient can think when he unwraps the gift: "She must really have been thinking about me when she wrapped this!" One person might need shortening, or sugar, or enough yarn to make a large sweater, while for another a small calendar would be just right. The wrapping is unimportant on an ordinary package, for the important thing is the content. But a proper Christmas package must still look wonderful and mysterious after the outer mailing layer has been taken off. Evergreen branches very often don't survive a long trip very well, but the shimmer of stars and the magic of bright ribbon and paper are more durable, and the right words are best of all. In fact, a carefully-written letter can often be a complete, satisfying gift in itself. Often even a Christmas greeting which the children have colored, or a motto for the entire family inscribed on a selected calendar page, can be just right when wrapped with loving care.

While you are doing this, take an occasional look at your cradle scene, for it was because of that story from Bethlehem that we celebrate Christmas, and our presents should be only little reflections of its great joy. Last of all, let us think about one more kind of Christmas present, a kind which creates two-fold happiness. You must have a friend who is not indifferent to all the kinds of need there are in the world, someone who would be sure to understand when he receives a letter from you worded somewhat like this: "This year I want to give you a present for someone who needs it more than either you or I . . ." And then go on to tell as exactly as possible where this present is to go and what it is to accomplish, so that the other person can really participate in the joy of this gift. Your friendship may be deepened by the trust and freedom you display in giving this kind of gift.

First
Saturday
in
Advent

Tomorrow is Sunday, and before it comes, something new should be added to the nativity scene you have begun: it ought not remain empty of people any longer. One of the children will be glad to help you select a place for the trumpeter. Place him so that he can be heard far and wide, so that he can proclaim to everyone that this is not just any pasture, but a very special place, that something marvelous is happening here, to which they must all be witnesses. Now is also the time to put the cow and the donkey into their stalls. Give them some finely-cut straw for bedding and some hay for food. Perhaps you will even have a little feed-rack into which you can put it for them. You'll find that it is not hard at all to glue one together out of little sticks.

Wouldn't it be a nice idea, too, for you to put some little surprises under the pillows of both big and small in your family? That should really be a part of every Advent Sunday. Each of them will enjoy finding something "special": a sprig of evergreen and a cookie, for instance. And if you want to add something, why not write a little motto or verse for each of them? You say you've never done that before? But why shouldn't you do it now for the first time? It is better than any fancy card, for you have written it yourself.

From our childhood days we remember Luther's hymn:

Ah, dearest Jesus, holy Child,
Make thee a bed, soft, undefiled,
Within my heart, that it may be
A quiet chamber kept for thee.

16

In those days we used to be sure that the Christ Child would find a better, warmer bed with us than on hay and straw. Since then we have come to see that our heart is anything but a "soft, undefiled" bed. We ourselves know better than anyone else how restless, hard, and fickle our hearts are.

The Son of God did not come just into the poverty of the stall. He also came to the poverty of the spirit of the people of Israel, a proud and presumptuous people living in bondage to legalism. They were not exceptional people who had deserved the coming of God's Son. The invitation of that hymn, "Make thee a bed, soft undefiled," becomes our fervent prayer today: "O Lord, you who were patient with the people of Israel, who endured being laid on hay and straw, you are able to do what men cannot do, you are able to put up with me. Take my restlessness, my vain self-confidence, my insecurity, my envy, my coldness, my moodiness, my troubles, my fault-finding—take them all and surround them with your peace, that I may never forget you."

From Christmas on, new laws come into effect. In our everyday speech we say, "When you have improved yourself, when you have come to terms with your place in life, when your heart has become quiet and serene, when you have stifled your envy and your temper, when you have been made beautiful through your purity and meekness, *then* I will try to get along with you." There is only One who is willing to put up with smallness of spirit, lack of faith, and inner turmoil, and this One really is willing. How good it is for a difficult child who would like to be different, but just can't achieve it, when there is someone around who neither scolds him nor laughs at him, but simply makes himself available. Such a child is happy and at ease because he has a companion in his troubles.

"Make thee a bed, soft, undefiled"—whoever prays this children's prayer as an adult gains a companion for his life. He sees more hope for himself, and is no longer so completely at the mercy of his own nature, nor so tempted by people and things.

Second Sunday in Advent

O Come, O Come Emmanuel, shown on the opposite page, has an interesting and checkered history. It began in about the ninth century with seven antiphons called the "Great O's." The word antiphon suggests that the lines were sung alternately by two groups of singers; the name "Great O's" comes from the fact that each antiphon begins with "O." Sometime later, perhaps in the 12th or 13th century, a revision was made by an anonymous hymn writer. He took these seven texts, discarded two, changed the order of the remaining five, and made them into a hymn with an added refrain. The net result was this beautiful Advent hymn, which is a favorite of many.

O Come, O Come, Emmanuel

VENI EMMANUEL. 88, 88, 88.

Medieval Antiphons
Latin Hymn, 1710
Tr. John M. Neale, 1818-1866

Plainsong Melody, Mode I

Flowing

1. O come, O come, Em - man - u - el, And ran-som cap-tive
2. O come, O come, thou Lord of Might, Who to thy tribes, on
3. O come, thou Rod of Jes - se, free Thine own from Sa - tan's
4. O come, thou Day-spring,come and cheer Our spir-its by thine
5. O come, thou Key of Da - vid, come, And o - pen wide our

Is - ra - el, That mourns in lone - ly ex - ile here
Si - nai's height, In an - cient times didst give the law
tyr - an - ny; From depths of hell thy peo - ple save,
ad - vent here; Dis - perse the gloom - y clouds of night,
heaven-ly home; Make safe the way that leads on high,

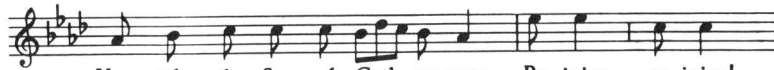

Un - til the Son of God ap-pear. Re-joice, re-joice!
In cloud, and maj - es - ty, and awe. Re-joice, re-joice!
And give them vic-tory o'er the grave. Re-joice, re-joice!
And death's dark shad-ows put to flight. Re-joice, re-joice!
And close the path to mis - er - y. Re-joice, re-joice!

Em - man - u - el Shall come to thee, O Is - ra - el!
Em - man - u - el Shall come to thee, O Is - ra - el!
Em - man - u - el Shall come to thee, O Is - ra - el!
Em - man - u - el Shall come to thee, O Is - ra - el!
Em - man - u - el Shall come to thee, O Is - ra - el! A-men.

One of our Lord's most beautiful names is the name *Emmanuel*. As St. Matthew's Gospel tells us, *Emmanuel* means "God with us." In our daily Christian life, this is our prayer and this is our joy. When Jesus comes we have the richest blessing of all. In Jesus our Savior we have "God with us."

Second
Monday
in
Advent

Isn't it true that every Christmas makes us at the same time happy and sad? It makes us happy that people think of us with love, that we ourselves can bring about some happiness, simply because that wonderful, familiar festival is here again. But there is something missing somehow. Perhaps we notice it on the morning of Christmas Day as we are straightening up the living room. The smell of candles and pine branches is still in the air, the presents are lying there, and we still seem to hear the happy shouts of the children. Was it really Christmas? For us personally? Maybe we had it arranged so that the Christmas tree was lighted just as the radio began playing Christmas carols, and with the playing of "Silent Night" we had warm and festive feelings in our hearts. We went to church. But how much of that spirit remains? Have we really met the Child of the Manger?

"Let us go over to Bethlehem, and see this thing that has happened." That is what the shepherds said to one another after they had heard the angel's message. Then they hurried to see Mary, Joseph, and the Child. That is what we, too, must do if it is really to be Christmas. For the children, the way to the Child in the Manger is often obstructed by Santa Claus, dime-store golden angels, and fascinating stories. For us adults it is the loads of work, the Christmas shopping rush, and the daily grind of our own lives which lie like a mountain between us and Christmas joy. This restlessness of our hearts, this bondage to the cares of the moment, make it almost impossible for us to come to the place where Christmas really happens, but we continue to long for it fervently.

Many before us have felt this same longing. They, too, had obstacles to overcome. In their desire to experience Christmas many of them have found ways to this Child. Until just a few years ago, Tyrolean farmers celebrated in this way: The entire family would stand in front of the manger scene and sing all the carols they knew, which was a great many. When they had finished the last one they left for their midnight Christmas service. The very small children, who were not able to walk the long way to the church, were given a special treat in the kitchen, but even for them the main thing was the joy shared before the Christmas manger. And let no one suppose that it was a trifling joy.

Perhaps you will say: "Oh, yes, but my husband and my children are different. We certainly can't imitate those Tyrolean farmers any more, today." This suggestion was not meant in that way. We do not need to do away with presents or with the Christmas meal, either. However, we could take one little step in a new (but also very old) direction: that of making the joy of Christ's birth in Bethlehem once more the central thing. This year it could be only a little thing like this: Go and choose one really good Christmas card and buy one for each member of the family who will be present on Christmas Eve. Then put them all away except one, which you can hang in the kitchen, or in the hall, or over the sofa in the living room, or where it can be seen easily. Don't say anything about it, but enjoy your plan quietly. When Christmas comes, every one of your dear ones will be presented with this same card which has accompanied the family through Advent. Doesn't sound like much, you say? We will do it at our house again next year, and perhaps something else like it in addition. For all of us really enjoy it, even if we do not say much about it.

Second
Tuesday
in
Advent

H as it ever happened to you, as it has to me, that even while you were buying it, the present which you had so carefully selected for a certain person suddenly began to seem small and "far too little"? Or have you lost sight of the real value of what the clerk is suggesting, and then later found yourself regretting having spent too much money?

The Winters family, for example, really had intended to buy building blocks for their little boy, blocks out of which he could build railroads, cities, and bridges. The girl in the toy department suggested "the latest thing," a tank. So on the evening of Christmas Day Mother must watch her little boy as he restlessly rolls his noisy, fire-spewing tank over his sister's dolls. How much better to have bought him the blocks, she thinks. It would probably have been better for *him*, too. Because newness often seems more important than rightness, it is important in our shopping that we both carefully ponder our decisions and stick to them.

Another thing you'll need is a list of all the names you want to remember, together with the thing you have chosen for each one. Here again the same principle applies as for the packages: not the quantity is important, but the thought you give to it. Consider individual needs and who could most benefit by knowing that you have thought of him. Do you have something for the postman who climbs the stairs for you every day? For the girl at the bakery? She has everything, you say? Certainly, she is able to buy herself many things, but in which shop can she buy a gift lovingly given? What are you giving Mrs. X? She is always unfriendly; never once will she greet you first. But then, how could she be cheerful—she is alone. No one ever "recharges her batteries" of goodwill and love. Perhaps an invitation to visit you early in January would be a marvelous gift for her.

Children catch the spirit of such plans very quickly. They volunteer to take over from that grumpy landlady the task of spreading sand on the sidewalk in front of the house. Father secretly decides to cheer up his unfriendly associate at work with one of his favorite cigars, and even to invite a slightly exasperating sister-in-law again during the holidays. When you think about such things, you come to realize that smiles, warmth, and trust are also important gifts. Genuine love for others stimulates our imaginations to think of the right gifts for neighbors and loved ones. So this list must not be written out in a hurry. You must be willing to give it thought, perhaps striking out something tomorrow and substituting something else.

The sense and center of all this is Christmas itself. Now, while it is still Advent, wouldn't it be nice if your husband and children could each receive another little token of love? Secretly they are longing for it. You say that can't be right, for everything is going so smoothly at your house? Cookies are being baked, friends invited, and the special Christmas dinner planned. The house is sparkling clean. You have even managed to help your husband answer some of the Christmas letters. And his best shirt will be ready for him, beautifully ironed. Everything is done so well that he certainly must notice . . . yes, what will he notice? Your self-giving, or only your efficiency? Don't be too efficient. It is better to leave something undone occasionally and really listen to him. Or "lend" the children to Grandma for once, put on your best outfit, and go with him to the movies. There *are* some good films now and then. Oh, yes, and take your time saying goodnight to the children this evening. Perhaps you yourself had a mother who often wanted to do that, but seldom got around to it. When she did come, however, it was wonderful, and you thought of a thousand devices to keep her from leaving. Things like these are not forgotten so easily, either by the little or by the grown-up children. This, after all, is the right time of the year.

Second
Wednesday
in
Advent

At the store or from a gardener we can get a few evergreen branches to bring home. There are many who like to put a sprig behind every picture in the room. The kitchen also would look the better for a little such decoration. If that seems too much for you, simply put one behind the best-loved picture. A few needles may fall off in the passage of time, but they can be picked up. Of course these unusual decorations are not meant to remain longer than over Christmas. They do add something to the whole house with their pleasant fragrance. All who come in enjoy them, even if they appear not to.

Today we will put the angel with the outspread wings into our manger scene. Then ask your little one what is new in it. The angel should stand in a conspicuous place and point toward the crib. And perhaps the sheep with the raised heads could stand and lie near him. They have become restless, and they are no longer eating and sleeping. They look up, noticing that something extraordinary is happening.

According to the Christmas story, one angel came first, and then came the heavenly hosts. Over the earth rang their great song of praise: "Glory to God in the highest, and peace on earth. . . ." Peace. That is a difficult word: many are painfully offended by it. You cannot but think of the last war and the wounds which it left. Already there is concern and fear of a new war. Then what has been changed by the coming of Jesus? The world goes its wicked way the same as ever. In those days, too, things went on as usual. The Roman emperor Augustus carried out his policies and sent out his decrees. Mary and Joseph, too, had to obey his authority. Cyrenius the governor had no idea that in the little town of Bethlehem, which belonged to his jurisdiction, something earth-shaking would happen. Nor did the people of Bethlehem themselves notice anything; for them the Holy Night was a night like any other.

Nevertheless, things did become different. "To you this day a Savior is born!" In the endless succession of days there was one on which this was said for the first time. "Today" was the word they used. Ever since, there is no day on this earth, be it ever so dark, which is without this Savior. Jesus' manger bed stood on this earth, the world in which we were born and will die. His feet have trod this earth, the earth over which hundreds of thousands of people today run, walk, or stumble along with wounded feet. How close he is especially to them! For he was born away from home, and his mother had no place to lay him.

So it is that everything which we now are and do is bound up and related to him, and the world would no longer be the world without the word which he spoke. He can meet us anywhere. Again and again his peaceful voice pierces through all of the moaning and cursing and empty talk of men: "Blessed are . . . the persecuted . . . those who hunger and thirst after righteousness . . . the pure in heart . . . the peacemakers . . . the merciful. . . ." Often it seems as if an insurmountable dark wall were placed between God and us. But Christmas tells us that this wall is really as thin as a breath. Wherever we are Christ suddenly appears and says, "Peace be with you!"

Second
Thursday
in
Advent

In a book I found a letter written by a prisoner of war, and in reading it I have grasped anew that there is a happiness which cannot fade away. Because this happiness is here attested by men who have experienced it while in the deepest valley of the shadow:

December 25, 1947

". . . No day is harder for the prisoner than Christmas Day. But some lines out of my mother's last letters have moved me deeply. I shall try to pass them on to as many of my comrades as I can. 'At Christmastime the hardest things in our lives cannot become harder, but easier; for we know only him from whom everything comes and to whom everything leads, and he is with us every day. Without Christmas everything would be intolerably hard; but whoever hears about Christ as Christmas will have a lighter, not a heavier heart.' Because of the shortage of hymnbooks we have done what we do for every service—written the songs for Christmas out by hand, and none sounded as triumphant as Paul Gerhardt's 'Come, and let us honor Christ . . . we, who know him conquer sorrow.'

". . . Anger and disappointment were great. Once more the day of our release had been pushed into the indefinite future. The camp authorities had stated their opposition to all Christmas celebration except one service, to which our comrades came in large numbers. As I was walking to the barracks in which our Christmas Eve observance was to be held together with our Roman Catholic brothers, I heard a young Swabian say in an outburst of complaint to the man beside him: 'Everything is so senseless, so senseless!' And it certainly was just that. Not only our fate here, but everything, yes, everything in the world seemed without meaning. And yet everything in the world, including our fate here, became meaningful and full of abiding purpose through Christmas, through the 'hour of salvation' in which eternal life came to be bound up with our poverty.

"Why did I walk by and leave him there in his desperation leaning on the wall, instead of taking him along with us to our service? Many times I have been able to take hold and say the right word, but this time I went by him heavy and powerless, like the priest and the Levite along the road to Jericho. And when I think back on it now, I realize that precisely here lies our commonest and most terrible guilt. We enjoy the Gospel instead of proclaiming it; we pass by the man who is desperate because he does not know the Gospel and expects nothing from it. . . ."

We should not wait until we meet someone who is desperate. There is certainly someone in the neighborhood whom we could speak to and bring to our home. It should be so much easier for us than it was for the man who wrote that letter. Nevertheless, we also have our shyness to overcome. Just be confident, for an angel goes with you on such missions. Perhaps you will drink coffee together. Don't allow that to be all, however. In the presence of the crib or of burning candles the most unmusical have been known to sing. Choose a well-known Advent hymn for the first one. Let the children be there with you. In these weeks such things go much more easily than usual.

Second Friday in Advent

Countless pictures have been painted of Jesus' birth in the manger, but very few depict the event in Palestine as it probably actually happened. Most artists have transferred it to their own homeland, to the mountains of Tyrol or into an industrial city in the Ruhr. Of course, that holds true everywhere, not only in Germany and Europe. In China the Child has narrow, slanted eyes, and his mother holds him with delicate little hands. In Africa it is a black child, and a Negro mother is shown giving him a banana. Instead of the Wise Men, the tribal chiefs come and bring him as a gift a large, painted drum. This is perfectly in order; the essential thing is that all grasp that Christmas comes into our world today.

There is one thing which many such pictures have in common: over the crib hangs a cross. We are almost ready to protest at that. Why must every joy be extinguished immediately? Why should there be a note of seriousness in this happiness? We certainly know that we have not earned God's goodness to us. But now that he has given it to us, why should we not simply rejoice? Lent will soon enough set before our eyes the picture of death and suffering.

Bethlehem's manger, in which God gave us his Son, is only the beginning. If it were complete in itself God's message would have to sound like this: "I am sending you my Son. His presence, his words, and his way of living will help you walk in a new way." And then? Then we would be lost in spite of all. We all know how many new beginnings and good intentions there already have been in our lives. Have we ever succeeded in keeping just one of them in love, in patience, in continuing determination to be as thankful and joyous as on the Sunday we made the resolution? How often we have wanted to celebrate Christmas the way it ought to be celebrated, and yet we find ourselves still just playing with external things. But God does not only make a beginning, he carries it out to a successful conclusion. This good ending for us means a criminal's death for the child in the manger. He stood in that place where the guilty man stands. In all the judgment places of this world he stands in the place of the condemned. Wherever men accuse us he steps in front to shield us. Even when our own hearts accuse us he says, "I have borne the penalty, so you need not." And when God raised his arm to hurl fiery destruction at selfish mankind, his own Son, born of a woman, received the blow and was killed.

The cross which shadows the happily laughing child in the crib is also the cross of a man who dies in agony, and it alone is able to fulfill our joy. God does not only give us a new chance or simply grant us another try. He forgives our sins through the death of his Son. The cross over your cradle scene is saying to you: God will never give you up.

Second
Saturday
in
Advent

Today is Saturday and tomorrow Sunday. And how much preparation is still left to be done! I do not know you, but I consider it possible that you are an excellent housewife, and that today you are
concentrating all your energies on fixing your house just right for
your loved ones. That is perfectly fine, as long as you observe the
rule: you must run the house, and not the other way around. Yes,
spare yourself some of the darning and patching until January, decide that perhaps the windows need not be polished once more nor
the entire house completely cleaned again. Nor would the floor have
to be waxed again—the children, after all, would soon have it scuffed
up again. During the Advent and Christmas seasons a house should
certainly be festive, but it need not be as dazzlingly clean as an
operating room!

You see, I would like to encourage you to practice even a little
more freedom: go to church tomorrow. Don't let your preparations
and cares keep you from it. Don't you think it would be good for
your troubled heart and harried mind? If you have to go alone it
will be good for the children to learn that there are times when
Mother is not there to satisfy their demands. This suggestion is
really not asking so much of you—and it will actually do them good
to see that there are things which are more important than we ourselves. That church service tomorrow can be more important than
"togetherness" or a late family breakfast. And it would be best of
all if you could go as a family.

If it simply can't be done, either alone or together, there is another possibility. Your Sunday can be more meaningful if you today

place the two shepherds into the nativity scene you are construct-ing. One is holding his hand to shield his face from so much heav-enly glory, the other (standing a little farther back) happily spreads his arms wide, as if he could in this way better seize and hold all this happiness.

Tomorrow, before the radio or television brings the church serv-ice, see to it that the table is cleared. You could light three of the Advent candles, and perhaps put your special Advent card with them. Everyone should sit quietly during this half hour and look at these things.

This quiet time on Sunday morning is a gift to you from God himself. He knows how much you need it. For once your hands can lie very still you should not have to be doing anything except listening and receiving. God will help you to make this service what it should be. And you do very much need his help, now more than ever. How much is expected of a mother at a time such as this, and especially if she is a Christian! She ought both to be happy herself and to be able to bring happiness to others. At least she should not upset the peace of the household by impatience and nervousness. There is hardly ever a time when the list of "Christian responsibilities" is as long and detailed as right now, and never is individual failure more bitter! The wonderful thing is that God does not meet our human needs and pitiful failures with cold and un-sympathetic demands, but with mercy. The last thing he wants is that our remembering of the coming of his Son should in any way become burdensome for us. Rather he wants to lay his own hand on us, so that we, his children, might once more really be happy, today and tomorrow and every new day.

31

Third Sunday in Advent

Paul Gerhardt has been called the "Prince of Lutheran Hymnists." More of Paul Gerhardt's hymn-texts have found their way into the English language than those of any other German hymn writer, including Martin Luther. The greatness of Paul Gerhardt's texts is attested to by the fact that as years go by they become increasingly popular and meaningful. In spite of a sad and troublesome life, Paul Gerhardt was filled with a glorious spirit which spills out in his poetic utterances. His hymn, *"O how shall I receive thee,"* shown on the opposite page, is based on Matthew 21:1-9, one of the Advent Gospel texts.

O How Shall I Receive Thee

ST. THEODULPH (VALET WILL ICH DIR GEBEN). 76, 76. D.

Paul Gerhardt, 1607-1676   Melchior Teschner, 1584-1635
Tr. Composite

Vigorously

1. O how shall I re - ceive thee, How greet thee, Lord, a - right?
2. Thy Zi - on palms is strew - ing, And branch - es fresh and fair;
3. Love caused thine in - car - na - tion, Love brought thee down to me;
4. Re - joice then, ye sad - heart - ed, Who sit in deep-est gloom,

All na - tions long to see thee, My hope, my heart's de - light!
My heart, its powers re - new - ing, An an - them shall pre - pare.
Thy thirst for my sal - va - tion Pro - cured my lib - er - ty.
Who mourn o'er joys de - part - ed And trem - ble at your doom,

O kin - dle, Lord most ho - ly, Thy lamp with - in my breast,
My soul puts off her sad - ness Thy glo - ries to pro - claim;
O love be - yond all tell - ing That led thee to em - brace,
He who a - lone can cheer you Is stand-ing at the door;

To do in spir - it low - ly All that may please thee best.
With all her strength and glad-ness She fain would serve thy Name.
In love all love ex - cel - ling, Our lost and fall - en race.
He brings his pit - y near you, And bids you weep no more.

33

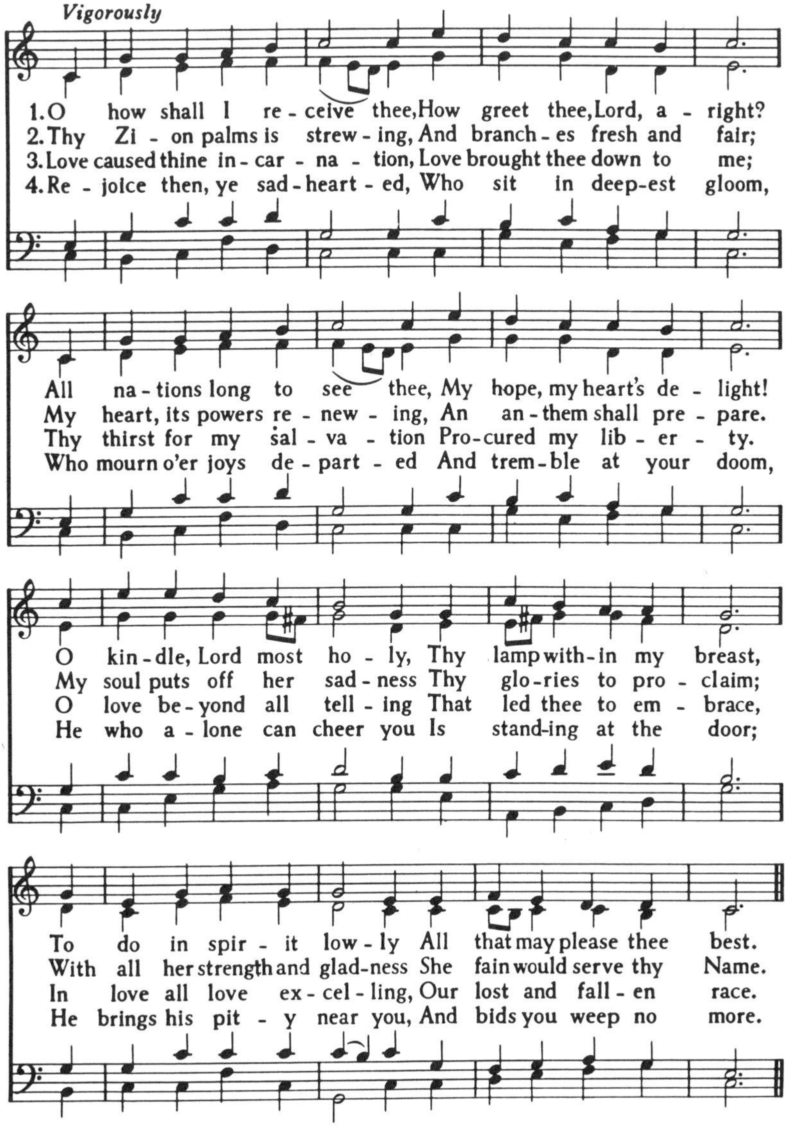

Third Monday in Advent

Isn't it remarkable how much can depend on what kind of words we use to greet those who come to our door? Consider these: "Well, you're finally here!" "How we have waited!" "Oh, let me tell you about the trouble those neighbors gave me again today!" "Please take your shoes off first. Why do you insist on making more work for me?" "You've made me keep your dinner for you again!" The one who has come forgets everything he was about to relate or to comment about. It can be that he has again been thoughtless, but that certainly could wait until after dinner, if it has to be discussed.

Coming home seems a simple thing, but it seldom happens the way it should when the one who comes meets words like these. If a person knows in advance that he will get such a reception he will not come home gladly. Children would rather stay outside a little longer, and a husband always will be finding more reasons to come home a little later, and will look for warmth and understanding somewhere else. I know an older woman with many grown-up children, many of whom are already married. But she understands the art of welcoming them home. Each of them knows that she will be happy when they come. And how happy she is! Even though they sometimes come too early or too late and sometimes without giving her notice, her little home is seldom empty. Beginning with her first words of greeting it simply is good to visit her. This isn't something which she plans; it's just the way she is.

Perhaps things are not exactly that way in my home and yours. Why not try to make it that way today, beginning with the next

34

person who rings your bell? What if it is only another fellow taking donations for something? Yes, then too. He must earn a living too, and often the way the next hours go for you and your loved ones can depend on just some little thing like that. If perhaps you aren't successful the first time you try this, because you may be too temperamental or nervous, don't give up. There will be someone else at the door soon. If it is your little Stevie home from kindergarten with his lunch pail broken again, say something kind to him in spite of it. Try to think first of him, the child, before you think of yourself and of the lunch pail.

During Advent we seem to be better able to try out such new ideas. Why is that? Well, certainly radio, press, and television, as well as Christmas trees and neon lights, are bound to influence our attitudes somewhat. There is bound to be a more open, more lively spirit about. But does that add up to Christmas? What would the world be like if there were no Christmas? It would not mean only that a few days in the year would be a little poorer in sentimental feelings. If there were no Christmas it would mean that Christ had not been born. Then we would have to speak about a God-forsaken world of senseless toil, as do those who have lost all hope.

Christ *was* born. God has not forgotten the world, he has loved it. When the heavens opened over those shepherds and flocks God was once more revealing to us the love of his heart. We need not become weary. Because that happened, we can turn once more in love to the people around us. The angels and the multitude of the heavenly hosts, who can look deeper into God's actions than we, certainly knew what they were doing when they chose just that hour to begin their great song of praise: "Peace on earth, good will to men."

Third
Tuesday
in
Advent

It won't be long now until Christmas. In the panorama of our nativity scene there is more and more activity now. Today you must take someone with you to look at the scene. Then sit down, both of you, and ponder what place should be given to the walking shepherd and to the sheep who runs ahead of him. I would suppose that by now they ought to be very close to the crib, but you will have to see if that will work out in your scene. Children are usually very ready to try out different ideas of arrangement, while a grown-up tends to be a little hesitant at first. But that will take care of itself. If your little guest at the crib decides that it would be better to let the sheep follow behind the shepherd, and not run in front of him, then be happy with her decision and do it as she says. In this way you have again given someone else part of the happiness of building the cradle scene.

Today I wanted to tell about the shepherds. Originally all the figures had names. This one is "Urberl," or Urban. He could also be called Hansl or Dennis. He carries a rolled-up sheet under his arm, and is in a great hurry, for he would not want the holy Child's bed to be hard.

The mother holding her little boy's hand cannot walk as fast as that, and so she is farther away from the cradle. This mother and child has, as long as anyone knows, been called simply: "Mother, let me go with you!" Simple as this name is, it suggests so many experiences and thoughts. For us it is like a question: "Have you in these weeks opened your heart to the Child in the manger?" Perhaps you have been doing so very secretly, happy in the thought that no one will know, no one will be embarrassed. But there are hands stretching out to you which say, "Mother, let me go with you!" Your children and other children, even your husband—they all want to be taken by the hand and brought along.

God has been especially kind to mothers: he entrusted his own Son to one of them. God certainly could have found another way to bring his Son into the world. He would not have had to use mothers. Often fanciful artists have portrayed how flowers and other wonderful and beautiful natural things might have been the cradle of the Son of God. But God did not only give his Son to a world that instead deserved death—he entrusted him to a mother. What a wonderful proof of God's patience and forbearance! No era of history and no country ever will be able to honor the contribution of mothers as much as God himself did when he was so kind to Mary. Since that day when Mary said, "Let it be to me according to your word," every child which a mother is given is a new sign of God's promise. Even though wars and devastation break over a country, though rebellion and revolution ruin it, still there will come a new springtime over the land, a springtime with flowers and grass, and mothers again will bring children into the world, for God's work of creation will continue to go forward as long as he wills it. "While the earth remains, seedtime and harvest, cold and heat, summer and winter, day and night, shall not cease." So goes the promise which God gave the world in Genesis, but it is not limited only to the specific things which are mentioned. It applies to all human life which God gives and entrusts to mothers. Take your children with you on the road to Bethlehem.

Third
Wednesday
in
Advent

The welfare of those around us often depends a great deal on what we do and do not do, and this is true also at Christmas time. What we are doing is perhaps more important to them. I think that we must also remember the importance of *not* doing. My mother did not seem to know this. Perhaps no one ever laid a hand on her shoulder and advised her to rest a little. Then, I think, she might have done it. But no one did, and so she not only baked, fussed, and bought, she washed, cleaned, darned, and polished until late into the night. By Christmas Eve, Mother was so exhausted that she would fall asleep right in the midst of the joyful shouts of her children. Honestly, it will hurt no one if you lie down for half an hour's rest, even in broad daylight! If that simply is not possible, then cancel part of your plans for this evening, and go to bed a little earlier than you did last night. Try to repeat this on a few more of the days remaining before Christmas. It is easier to be loving when you have had your sleep. Christmas will be less drudgery and more like it ought to be if you are not dead tired, if you can really celebrate with the others, singing and laughing along, and taking an interest in the toys that the children lay in your lap.

Too, when you have had your sleep you will be better able to conquer the sighing discontent which so easily comes into a tired mind, and spoils your joy: "If I had my way, I'd abolish Christmas." "This is the worst time of the year; it's then I first notice how much I have lost." "How much better it was in the days when the children still believed in the Christ Child's coming!" When the

Christmas lights burn there is reflected in their glow all the good things of yesterday, all the happiness and love which people have given us. One person relives the Christmases of his childhood, another remembers how the family used to walk together to church for the Christmas Eve service. Still others think about the holiday cookies which Grandma used to make. All these memories take on new life in the candles of Christmas Eve. Our hearts become heavy with longing for the good things of the past. But if the season is not a blessing to us and only a burden, then all those are right who say, "It's better to keep on working and avoid thinking about it than to celebrate." Then the candles mirror only a false memory which destroys our Christmas joy.

There is a memory which is more than thinking back on happy times. It has continued through almost two thousand years. In the rise and fall of empires, in invention and progress, much has been forgotten and much has been lost. But the memory of God's action remains: "God so loved the world, that he gave . . . ." That is Christmas. Since then he lives among us, accessible even to tired and timid hearts.

The Apostle Paul wrote: ". . . that the eyes of your heart may be illumined." That is the right kind of remembering. With eyes lighted in this way one can then confidently look back. In the light of right remembering Christmas loses all of its distressing power to wring regretful sighs from us. For in the light of God's love, the people and places of the past—together with everything which is denied to us or made difficult for us—are no longer losses, but gifts of God. His acts toward us are gracious.

Third
Thursday
in
Advent

I wasn't a little child any more when this happened, but I still had to keep looking at the golden flecks on my finger. The enchanting color was still there, despite soap and brush. We had been painting nuts with golden paint. Even though you can buy almost anything nowadays, and often for amazingly little money, you ought to treat yourself and the children to the little ceremony of gilding the nuts for the Christmas tree. A little friend from school can be invited to help. We will need walnuts, darning needles, red wool yarn, a little can of gold paint from the hardware store, and a brush. The TV will have to be turned off and all the painters will sit down at the table, which has been covered with newspaper. One can stick the needle into the nuts and fasten on them the yarn with which they will be hung on the tree. The older ones can do the painting, and the littlest one gets the job of swinging them gently to dry. Finally, we will put out all the lights except one candle in front of the manger. The fact that it is dark in all the places which demand our work serves only to add to the brightness of the Christmas joy in that little circle of light. Then, when we have sung together, Stevie says that we ought to have a star for the stall in the nativity scene, so that on Christmas Eve, when Mary and Joseph and the Child have moved in, the Wise Men will be able to find them. There is just enough gold paint left in the can to make one.

What kinds of people do you suppose came walking to Jesus' cradle? Certainly many more kinds than we have to put into our scene. There must have been many there who never came to church, and about whom the others thought, "He should not pretend in that way; he ought at least to stay more in the background, and not press forward into the center!" But the Bible does say that God loved *the world*, not just a few chosen individuals. Jesus knew them all, and he met them, wherever they went. He thought about them all as he told the story of the royal wedding. With two of them he died on the cross. Doesn't that mean that his family reaches even to the poor, the uprooted, the failures? Yes, it reaches that far, however hard it may be for us to accept the idea.

I remember one Christmas Eve when there was a disturbance in the house next to us: the drunken father was beating his wife and children. "And on Christmas!" we said, in dismay. On another Christmas Eve there was loud singing in the apartment above us— but it was not Christmas music. Mrs. X had already explained it: good food and interesting guests were *her* idea of Christmas. Or we would pass a restaurant with an electric Christmas tree in its window into which people were streaming, and we would say with disappointment, "That is supposed to be Christmas!"

It *is* Christmas! We can be assured that all this which we see *is* Christmas. The Child of the manger does not come only to respectable families, not only to the circle around the Christmas trees and gathered in the churches, not only to those who think about Christmas and know how to keep it correctly. God's love extends over the whole world. It extends also over all the false observances, over guilt and over indifference. "God's Son has become your brother." Our brother—your brother—your brother and ours. We are together as we go, the respectable and the unrespectable, the pious and the doubting, the deeply troubled and the scornful. Thus receiving God's Christmas gift means this: not to separate ourselves from other men, whom he loves as well as he loves us.

41

Third
Friday
in
Advent

W hat was Christmas Eve like at your home when you were a child? Was the door simply opened, the candles lighted, and then each child went to open his presents? I am reminded of two boys who have never experienced Christmas any other way. Last year their parents secretly set up a toy electric train, timing it so perfectly that it started up just as the door opened. Both of them threw themselves joyfully on it and then (they are both still very young) began fighting and screaming because each wanted this beautiful toy for himself. The quarrel was patched up and the tears dried, but how much better this Christmas would have been if before the distribution of gifts the father had read the Christmas story, or if they had recited together some verses they had been preparing. The nativity scene ought to stand right in the middle of things, so that each one can see it easily.

> O little Child, I want to love you with all devotion,
> In joy and in sorrow I'll hold you in my heart.
> Let me never part from you. Bind fast the bond
> Of love between us, and take my heart as a token.

You say that a child cannot understand this, especially at such an exciting and long-awaited occasion. You are certainly right. But perhaps, as the years go by, he will begin to understand the meaning of "take my heart as a token." That is our response to God's Christmas gift to us.

We know that all other Christmas gifts are satisfying only when the recipient is truly happy over them and when he senses our love in our gift. We have all had the sad experience of having our gifts nullified by someone who either "checked them off" greedily or took no notice of them. Does the subtle rule that a gift becomes complete only when it is rightly received apply even to that overwhelming gift God gave us? Yes, even God's saving gift is perfected in our receiving it. This can take our breath away: God doesn't force anything on us, he offers it, Christmas after Christmas.

To receive means simply to leave him room in our hearts. Everything else of which our lives are full—needs, worries, plans, wishes, goals, and many unimportant things—must make way for him. The person who prays his childhood prayer, "May Jesus alone have a place in my heart," comes with a royal gift to the Child in the crib. Give him your heart! Just how to go about bringing him this precious gift will be different in each life.

Far from her children and grandchildren there lives an old, lonely woman. She has no one for whom she can prepare a Christmas celebration, but on Christmas Eve she decorates the table in her little home with pine branches and a lighted candle. Then she has her Christmas as she prays a prayer for each of her children and grandchildren. This continues until it is time to go to the festival midnight service. "Knowing that Mother is praying for us on Christmas Eve is the best Christmas present of all," says one of her daughters.

Giving him our heart means giving him our thoughts and time and money by devoting them to others. Perhaps it means giving up some of the usual ways of celebrating Christmas and having the courage to make the reading of the Christmas story the beginning of our family's Christmas. Now while there is still plenty of time, why don't you talk to your husband and ask him to read Luke 2:1-20 on Christmas Eve?

Third
Saturday
in
Advent

Right now everyone, including youth groups, homemakers' organizations, secretaries, sororities, and athletic clubs, is busy planning a Christmas party. There is hardly a group of people who will not have some sort of observance with a tree, singing of carols, and exchange of gifts. Some of them even re-enact the Christmas story, the story of Mary and Joseph and the shepherds in the field.

Once a long time ago I had the part of a shepherd in one of those Christmas plays. I am not a very good actress, but that made no difference there. We completely forgot the danger of saying our lines wrong, and that a hall full of people would be watching. On the stage stood a makeshift little cradle in which there burned a candle to signify the new-born Baby. All that happened in our performance was that we shepherds knelt down before the cradle and looked into the light of the candle. We had to kneel a long time. Finally the group sang a closing hymn with many stanzas. But we were not fully conscious of things around us; we were in Bethlehem with body and soul, lost in wonder at the greatness of God's gift.

I thought again about the experience today as I looked at the last shepherd in the box of figures for the creche—the kneeling one with the red jacket whose big hands are pressed together in joy and awe. Let us now put a light into our little home-made crib where the Baby will soon lie. Then let us have the oldest shepherd kneel before it and bring the little one in from the meadow, the one who has been shielding his eyes from the blinding light of the angel. He will have cause to shield his eyes here too.

Oh, yes, the shepherds came to the crib in the same way men

44

come to it today: cold through and through, frightened, shaken, and this not only from the hard battle of a difficult life and an uncertain age. In addition to all that, they had experienced a still greater fright. As the heavenly light suddenly broke over their heads in the night, as they suddenly saw themselves as poor little men standing in the midst of the Lord's radiant clarity, they came to see that the heavenly world, God's world, really exists: an inexpressible brilliance of light, untouched by our earthly darkness, unshadowed by the maze of hate, fear, pride and stupidity, out of which man finds no exit. Those who saw what the shepherds saw must first of all have felt a boundless despair. God is *that* holy, he is as pure as that heavenly light, and his world is a world of such radiant blessedness! How can our existence compare with it? There is no bridging that gulf, and no possibility for us to have a part in it. There all life turns on the jubilant praise of God, and here we circle in God-forsaken darkness. So they must have thought. "And they were filled with fear," we read. They went their way to the cradle fearful and afraid. But as they came away we hear that they were "glorifying and praising God." Between fear and praise came Christmas, the adoration of God's radiant life which came down to us, not for revenge or destruction, but for mercy, reconciliation, and blessing. "Look there and see how loving God is, how close he comes to lost mankind." Those who go to the cradle may go in fear, but when they return they praise him. All of us ought to be speaking this praise to one another much more than we do, and speaking about other things much less.

Fourth
Sunday
in
Advent

One day Joseph came home deeply troubled and said, "Mary, we must get ready to take a trip."

"Take a trip," asked Mary, shocked, "now, when I am about to have my baby?"

"Yes, now," said Joseph. "It is the command of Emperor Augustus. He wants to have those who live in his lands counted, and for that purpose everyone must go back where he was born. Therefore, I must go to Bethlehem."

Oh, how that troubled Mary! "What shall I do? The trip is so long, and I can take along so little! How will I get through this? Where will my baby be born?" Then she remembered the angel and his heavenly message. "It will be all right," Mary said bravely to herself, and set out on the journey with Joseph.

They could take only a very little with them, for it was such a long trip, and they had to go on foot. Into the mountains they climbed on steep and stony paths. Three long days they wandered. It was a cruelly tired Mary who finally entered Jerusalem's gate leaning on Joseph's arm. Now, they thought, we have almost made it. They stopped at a house and asked: "Could you take in two people?"

"Two people? Impossible—not even one. Everything's been full a long time."

They went farther, and asked again, but it was all in vain. Everything full, not a place anywhere. So the happiness of Mary and Joseph faded fast. Desperate and unhappy, they thought to themselves, "Something does not make sense here. Either God has for-

46

gotten us or it is not true that our child shall be a king, as the angel told us that time. For there certainly would have to be a place for a king to be born! But there was none. Finally, when they hardly dared to ask any more, someone took pity on them, and said, "Take a look back there in the stall; maybe there is room for you there." Like two poor forsaken fugitives Mary and Joseph fled to the stall, and it was there that Mary had to bring her little Child into the world.

Mary was alone with her Joseph. They had no help and nothing to ease the birth, not even a bed for the Child. It was fortunate that Mary had a few linen cloths along. In them she wrapped her little Son and then laid him in the manger out of which the cattle ate. It was hard for her, and in later years she many times thought back on it and wondered how it could be that God had left them so alone.

Then the door opens quietly, and men come in and look around. By their simple, weathered faces and rough clothing it is easy to see that they are shepherds. They look at the Baby, come quietly and carefully closer and look at the poor little Child in the manger. just as one looks at something especially lovely and precious. On their faces is a joy which is only rarely seen on the faces of men. Mary is amazed, and thinks: "What do they want here, and why are they so happy?" Reading her questioning eyes, they say to her: "The messenger of God came to us, and we heard from him that your Child is a King. Just think, all of heaven is rejoicing with you and with us! We have seen and heard how all of God's angels sang to honor this Child, sang because from this day the Lord can again love all people."

Oh, how happy Mary was over what the shepherds told her. All her weariness and dark thoughts were suddenly gone. Now she simply delighted in her Child, thrilled that he really was the King.

47